250 Continuous-Line Quilting Designs

for Hand, Machine & Long-Arm Quilters

Laura Lee Fritz

For Sally, Laura Lee Fritz

C&T PUBLISHING

This book is gratefully dedicated to the makers of over 12,000 quilts upon which I doodled my designs while learning how to draw these quilting designs. Thank you to Karen Nelson, Bernice Townsend, Meg Blau, Carolyn Griffin, and Cathryn Zeleny for producing some quilted samples of these designs. Thanks to Ron Paul for keeping me swept off my feet.

Attention Teachers:
C&T Publishing, Inc. encourages you to use this book as a text for teaching. Contact us at 800-284-1114 or www.ctpub.com for more information about the C&T Teachers Program.

Library of Congress Cataloging-in-Publication Data
Published by C&T Publishing, Inc.
P.O. Box 1456
Lafayette, California 94549

Fritz, Laura Lee.
  250 continuous-line quilting designs for hand, machine & long-arm quilters / Laura Lee Fritz.
      p. cm.
  ISBN 1-57120-171-8
  1. Quilting. 2. Quilts—Design. I. Title: Two hundred fifty continuous-line quilting designs for hand, machine & long-arm quilters.
  II. Title.
  TT835 .F756 2001
  746.46'041—dc21
                                  2001002357

Printed in China
10 9 8 7 6 5 4 3 2 1

Contents

What You Can Do with These Designs   4

Home & Garden   9

Birds   19

What You Can Do with These Designs

You can add beauty and special meaning to your quilting projects by using the graceful continuous-line images shown in the following pages. Whether you are quilting by hand, home sewing machine, or with a long-arm machine, this collection of designs will be a generous resource library.

You can combine them with each other and with interesting background-filling textures, as shown in the quilted samples.

Please enlarge or reduce any of the designs to use on your quilts, and feel free to arrange and combine these ideas with more of your own.

The Quilt Top as a Stage: Planning the Design

If you think of your quilt in terms of a stage, and the quilting designs as the actors on that stage, designing your overall quilting plan will be easy.

One design will act as the lead character on center stage, with a supporting cast of one or more secondary design ideas. Provide some backdrops, such as a background grid and some architecture, and your story will unfold.

Here are two examples.

Quilt a complete circle, and add another circle just inside to form a ring (the architecture).

Quilt a perched mourning dove (the lead character) (see page 26) just inside the ring, and add two lovely

The back of Dove Vest, *shown on page 34, illustrates the use of a lead character within a beautiful setting.*

blossoms (see page 43). Fill in the open spaces inside and outside the ring with a mix of woodland leaves (pages 31, 32, 41) and nuts. These form a backdrop.

Quilt a pair of deer (the lead characters) with a stream running in front of them (the stream can be formed by quilting a few vaguely parallel wavy lines). Add a ridge of tree-lined mountains (the secondary characters), and fill in behind the mountains with a backdrop of thunderclouds. For example, combine the top part of the cloudy landscape on page 73 with any or all of the deer figures on pages 60-61.

Not every quilt top needs such a complete drama. The quilting designs shouldn't upstage the patchwork. A traditional favorite like an Irish Chain needs some character and backdrop in the alternate blocks, and a "transparent" design in the patchwork blocks.

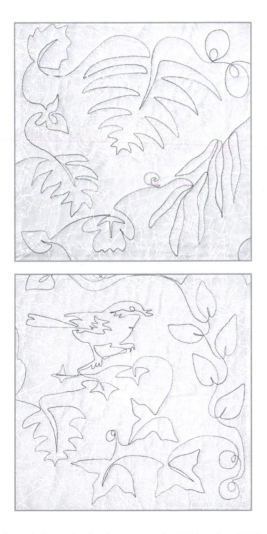

Details from the back cover quilt, A Woodland Tail, *are used in the alternate plain blocks.*

Another traditional favorite, the Log Cabin pattern, made with the 1930s reproduction fabrics currently available, is perfectly quilted using only the Baptist fan (page 74) or Orange Peel design (page 78).

Many of the nineteenth century reproduction fabrics are used in quilts now, and I often use a concentric teardrop (page 75) or paisley feather quilting design as they seem to be evocative of that era. In these examples, it is the era of the fabric that is the lead character; all we add by using these simple textures is the backdrop.

Some contemporary quilts don't require much added imagery to be effective. You can rely on a single texture in one color area, and a second texture for the other. For example, a "weaver fever" is a bargello of two color planes zigzagging across the quilt; I would choose a vertical/horizontal straight-line texture opposite a curvy-loopy texture to accentuate the change in direction. For a stack 'n whack quilt, quilt the background with one texture, and the pinwheel fabrics with another.

Transparent designs combine interesting shapes, but they are not made up of recognizable imagery. An overall meandering design is one example. Because of their simplicity, transparent designs don't jump out at you as you study a quilt. Other examples of transparent designs can be found in the textures section.

Some practice samples of transparent designs

You can also combine recognizable images with transparent designs; floating an occasional oak leaf on a still-waters texture is a subtle example of this blending of design ideas.

Sizing Your Designs

The primary design for a block should fill about two-thirds of the block. If the background is closely quilted, a recessed dimension will make the primary design stand out more clearly. A loosely quilted background with a highly detailed primary image will have the opposite effect; the background will puff up around the detailed image.

Negative Space

Unquilted areas of a quilt are referred to as negative space. Between your leaves and textures, for example, the blank shapes can be large or small, clumsy shapes or graceful. Be observant of them. A poorly balanced design will have a negative space that is confused with the image; a negative space can be so large that the quilt seems to be underquilted, or so small that the quilting lines are hard to interpret.

Hints for Repeated Images

When you repeat designs to create a row or border, connect the designs with part of your supporting or backdrop design. The quilted details on the jackets on page 35 are good examples of this treatment.

If you are planning a leafy border, avoid using a "row" of leaves. Create a more natural look by tilting each leaf in a different direction. Varying the size—or shape—of the leaves will help them fit within the space of the border, and will make the design less static.

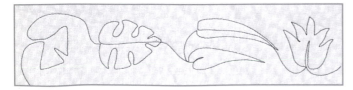

A row of leaves in varying directions looks more natural.

Transitional Quilting Lines

When you are planning the background design for the borders, consider "crossing the lines" into the quilt block area. This creates a smooth transition between the two areas, and you can work all your side borders as you progress down the quilt. The quilt on page 33 provides a good example of crossing the lines.

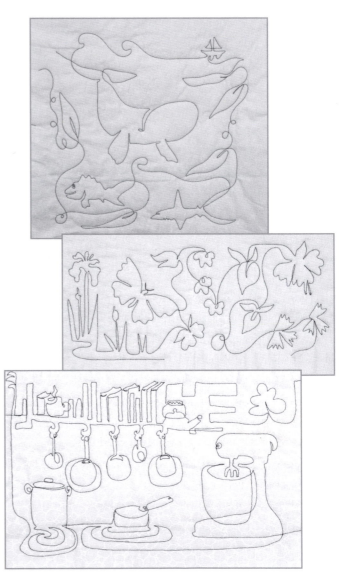

Keep transition and escape routes in mind; they need to be consistent with the shape or feel of the background quilting in order to remain invisible.

Transferring the Designs

If you aren't ready to make the leap into free-motion quilting, there are simple steps to follow to transfer the designs onto your quilt top.

1. Trace the designs onto paper with a black permanent pen so you can use a copy machine to resize any image for your block or border. Trace the tracing again onto stencil plastic and cut it out with a "hot knife."
OR
Trace the design onto bridal illusion (tulle), which is available at most of the larger chain fabric stores. Both of these methods are a means to draw directly onto your quilt top with chalk, washout pencil, clean-erase pencil or a water/air-soluble pen.

2. You can also trace your designs onto water-soluble stabilizer with a water-soluble pen and quilt through it as the topmost layer of your quilt. Try the Solvy stabilizers made by Sulky®, or Dissolve™ from Superior Threads, as they really do wash out of the cloth. Trace the pattern onto a piece of the Solvy or Dissolve using a pencil that washes out for light-colored fabrics or a permanent pen for darker fabrics. Pin the drawing in place on your quilt; it won't need many pins because it won't move much. Because the medium is transparent, it will be easy to place the drawing where lines won't need to be sewn over bulky seam junctions. Sew directly on your pattern lines. Pull away the largest chunks of the plastic-like material, then mop up the remaining fragments with a wet piece of cloth or a damp scrap of batting. I prefer using the batting to mop up because it holds water, scrubs without roughing up your quilt top, and doesn't leave shreds of itself behind.

A warning: If you leave larger pieces of the Solvy or Dissolve on the quilt after wetting, they will turn to slime which dries on the quilt; the quilt will need a thorough washing.

3. Another option is to draw directly onto your quilt top with a washable marker. You will need a light source for this method.

Tip: A recycled sliding-window pane (still framed) or glass door panel from a shower enclosure will serve you well as a light table.

Lay this glass panel over a quilt frame or sawhorse set, place a light source such as a four foot fluorescent shop light below the "table." Now spread your quilt top on top of the glass and turn the light on.

Slide your drawings under the quilt, and position as desired.

It becomes evident that clean white paper and bold black drawing lines will project best through the cloth.

In time this tracing will train your eye and hand, and you can draw your own patterns to increase your collection.

Tools to Make Your (Quilting) Life Easier

Some materials and tools have been designed to make home-machine quilting easier. Here are a few you may find mentioned in the descriptions of the quilts in the gallery section of this book.

I use a wide variety of threads and needles, and feel that experimentation is the best way to decide your favorites. I recommend Harriet Hargrave's *Heirloom Machine Quilting* as a source of information for any supplies.

The tools for small machine quilting are many. The simplest "rule" to remember is that any of the modern threads can be used by choosing a needle to be larger than the thread so the thread won't get roughed up or overheated during its journey in and out of the fabric.

- You can use stenographers' rubber finger tips, or rubber-spotted cotton gloves; both provide a non-grip, non-slip contact with your quilt sandwich as you slide the quilt over the machine throat.
- I recommend cotton batting because it sticks well to cotton fabric, which allows for less basting. But be sure to follow the manufacturer's directions for the amount of basting you do.
- Sullivan and Sulky make basting adhesive sprays to hold your quilt layers together; use a light spray or you may get a sticky needle.
- Both the Flynn Multi Frame™ System and HandiQuilter solve the problems of holding the quilt layers so you don't get them pleated, and holding the layers so that you can smoothly move them under your sewing machine needle.

    Both systems have three roller frames to hold your quilt. You slide the quilt under your darning foot before closing up the end of the frames.

    To work larger patterns than will fit within the reach of your sewing machine throat you scroll your quilt along the rollers back and forth as you progress.

Most of the designs in this book are already the right size to work without scrolling.

John Flynn has a small frame and roller system for under $100 that stretches your quilt sandwich for an easy rolling freehand movement. You roll your quilt onto a set of wood rails—whatever length suits the project—and have about 4"-5" of quilt all along that length for your patternwork. This makes you think of small imagery, overall patterning, or quilting the imagery in segments—half of a dog image on one pass and the second half of the dog as you pass after re-rolling the quilt. Another convenience of this frame system is that your project can be quickly moved to lean against a wall out of the way, while still rolled in the frame.

HandiQuilter has a larger frame set-up plus wheeled tracks and cross tracks that you set your home machine onto; these create a small-scale quilting machine. You mount your quilt sandwich onto a quilt frame and direct your home sewing machine with your hands, rolling it along the tracks on the multitude of wheels. You still work in a small section, creating your designs in more than one pass because your quilting area is only as deep as your machine throat allows. This is a very well-made, sturdy tool, and it can be mounted on a table as a temporary set-up or screwed to a work surface for more permanence. This frame can also be detached from the support structure to set aside the project without unrolling the quilt.

The HandiQuilter allows you to roll your machine as you work, but you will still need to use your foot pedal and may want to arrange a method of attaching it to a wheeled frame also.

Start Quilting

You just need to practice machine quilting in order to find your rhythm, and learn to sew at a constant speed.

Warm-up Tip: Begin by tracing the designs with your fingertips to practice the paths, and you will learn to stitch many of them free-hand. This tracing makes the pattern a physical memory and helps you quilt more smoothly.

When you start or end a line of quilting, or when your top thread or bobbin is depleted, knot the end(s) of your stitching line and thread a needle with the thread tails. Use a long-eye sharp embroidery needle for the tail sewing so both threads will fit through at once. Try wrapping the pair of threads around the eye tightly, pinch the thread to hold the tiny loops as you withdraw the needle, then slip the eye over these tight little loops. Sew these ends by sliding the needle back along your quilting line, pull the needle out, bury the knot into the batting, and cut the tail.

Please Note: All designs featured in the black and white photographs can also be traced and used in your quilts.

Home & Garden

Cherry Tomatoes

Carrot

Peas

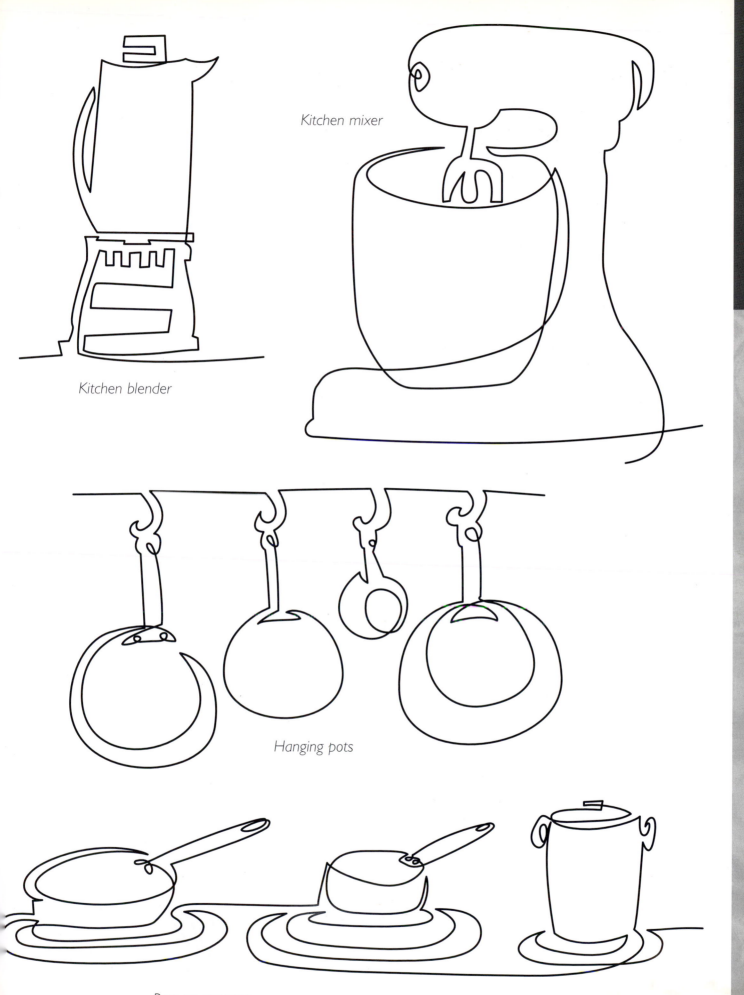

Kitchen mixer

Kitchen blender

Hanging pots

Pots on stovetop

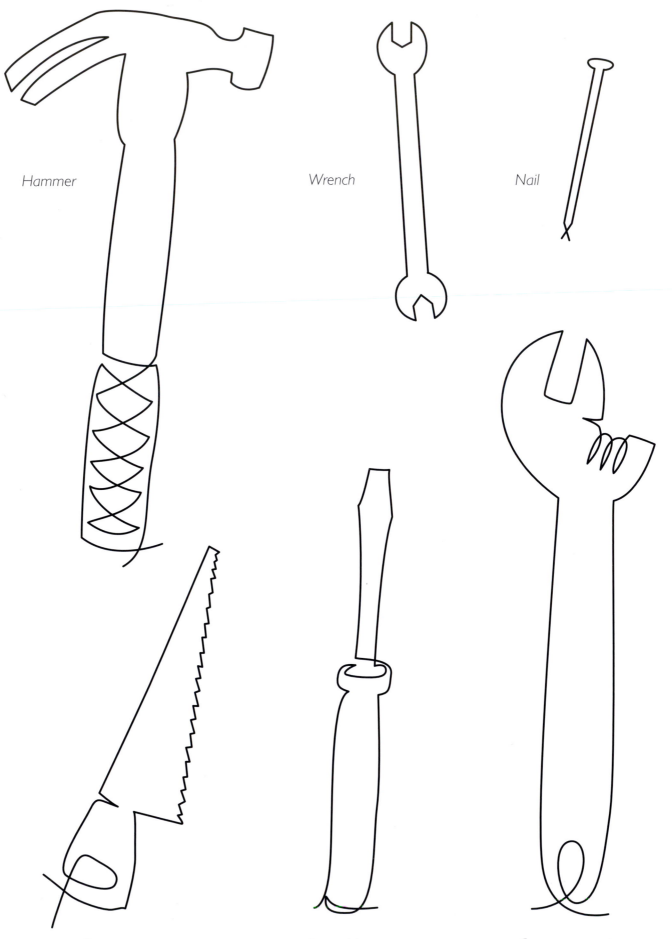

Hammer

Wrench

Nail

Saw

Screwdriver

Crescent wrench

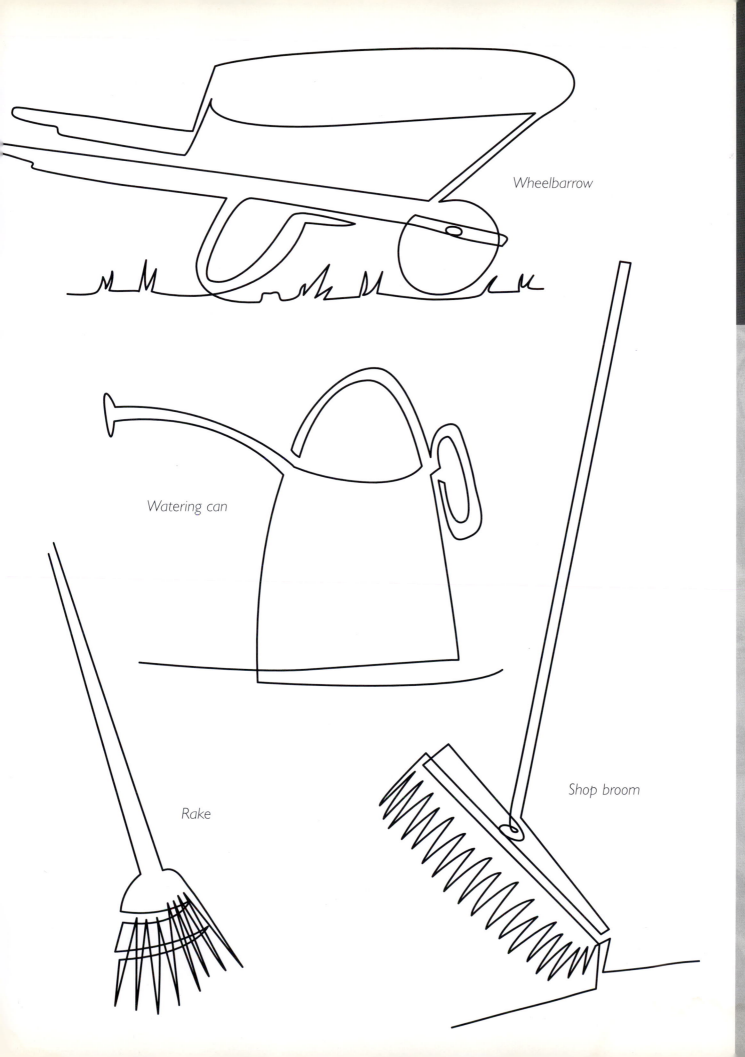

Wheelbarrow

Watering can

Rake

Shop broom

Mixing whisk and tea kettle

Steaming cup and saucer

Bowl and steaming mug

Pitcher

Coffeepot

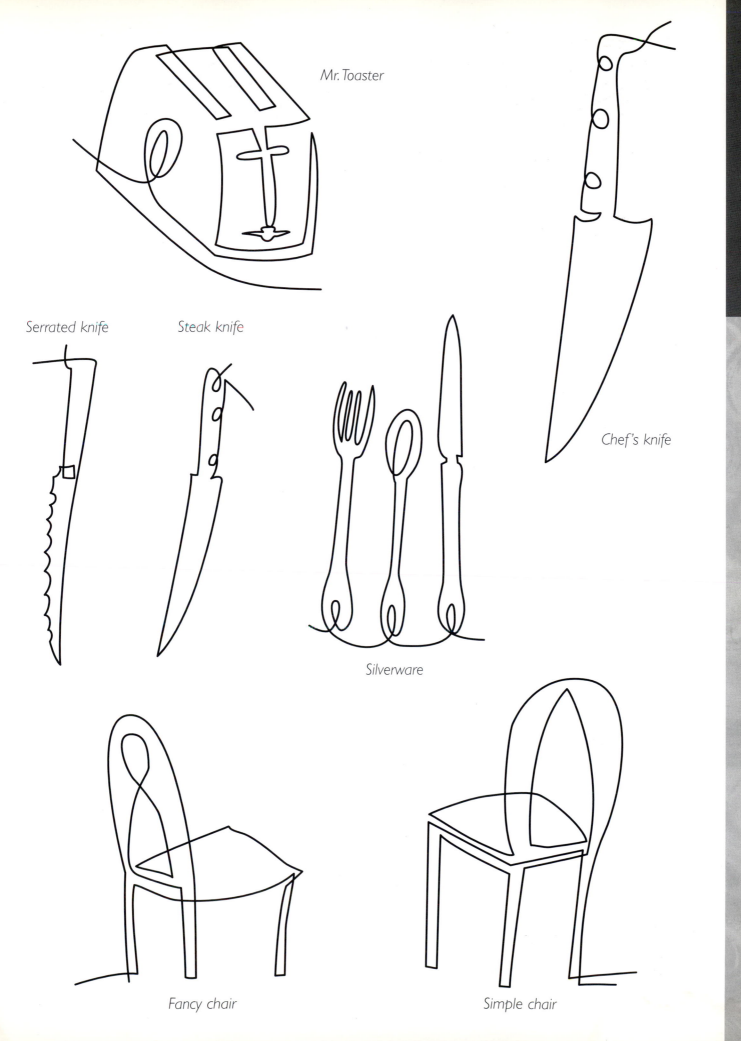

Mr. Toaster

Serrated knife

Steak knife

Chef's knife

Silverware

Fancy chair

Simple chair

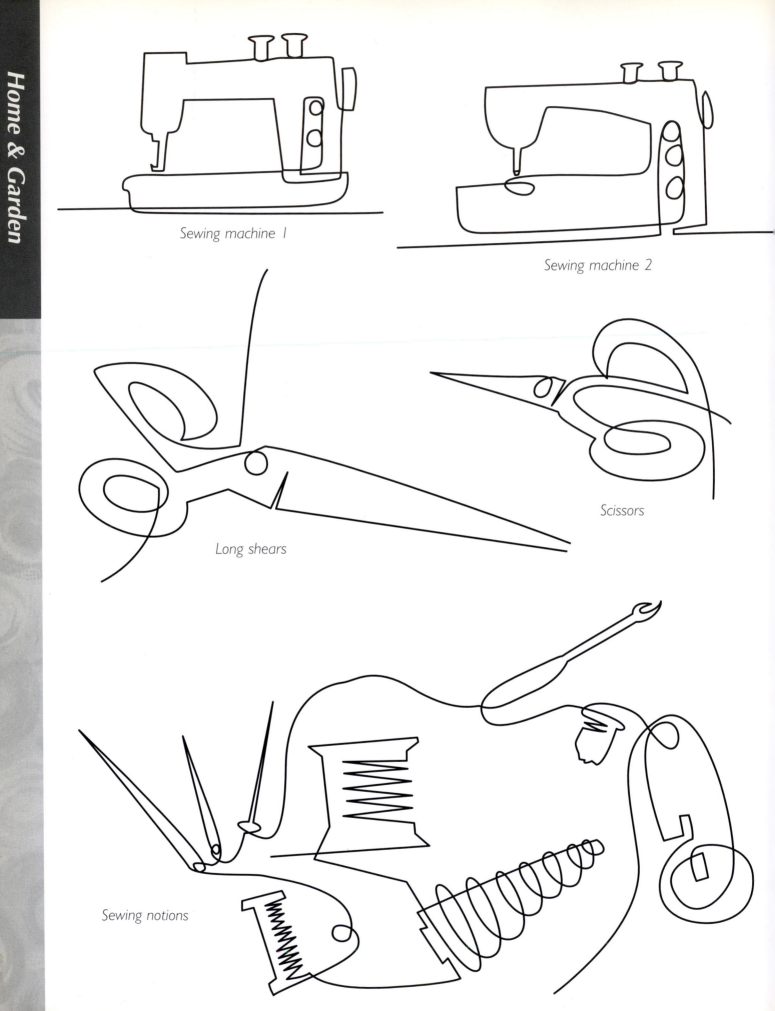

Sewing machine 1

Sewing machine 2

Long shears

Scissors

Sewing notions

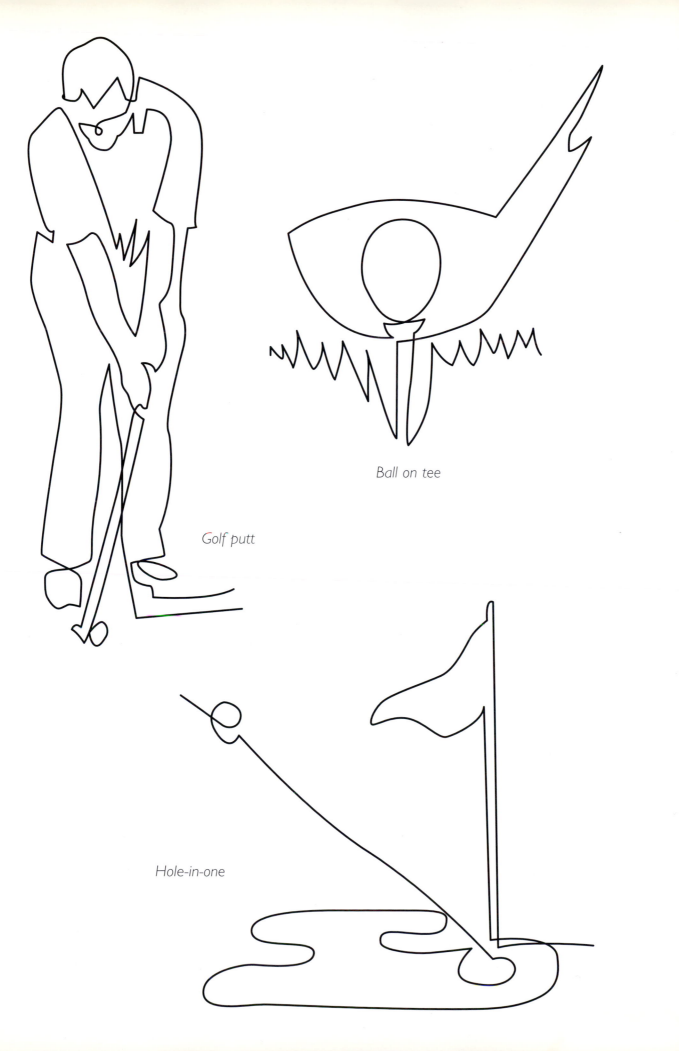

Ball on tee

Golf putt

Hole-in-one

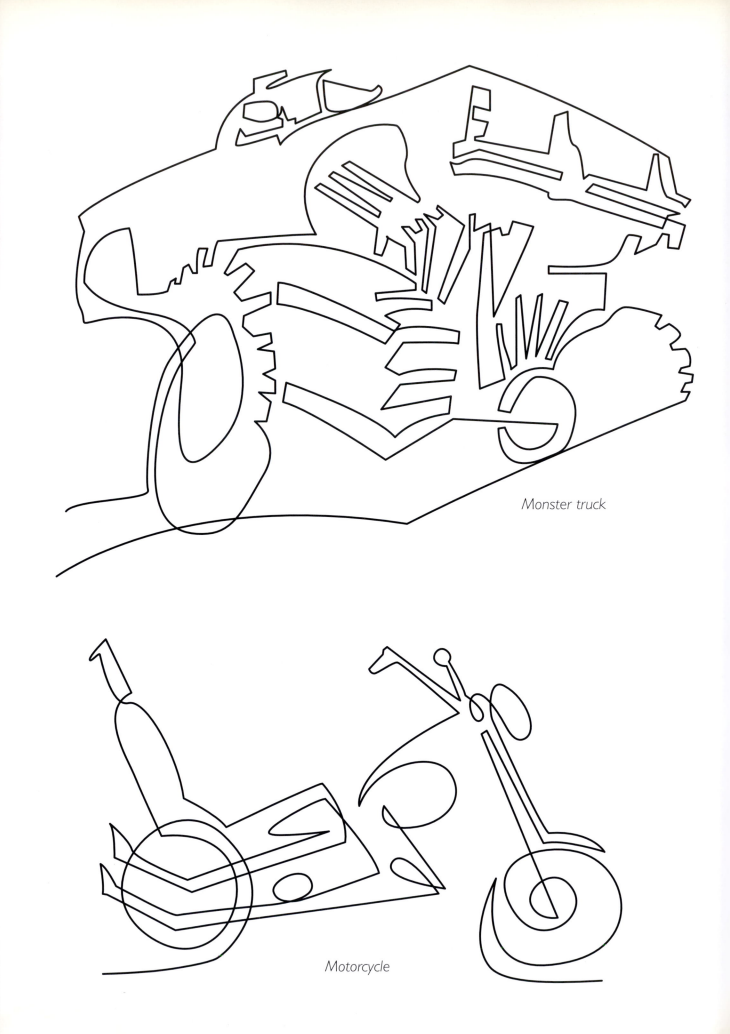

Monster truck

Motorcycle

Soccer players

Electric guitar

Basketball player

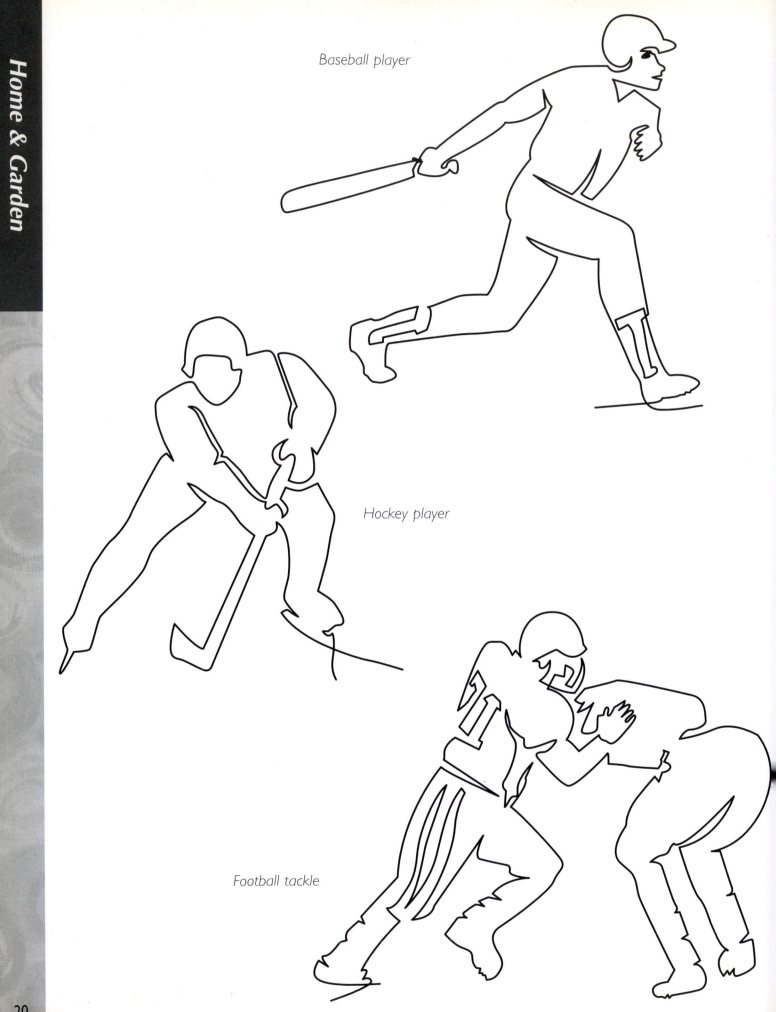

Baseball player

Hockey player

Football tackle

Birds

Nuthatch

Free-hand bird

Eagle with fish
over mountain backdrop

Pelican perched

Tall penguin

Penguin looking down

Pelican swimming

Penguin looking up

Tern flying in wispy sky

Chickadee

Jay

Feeding pelican

Walking bird

Blackbird flying

Blackbird

Adult quail

Pheasant in flight

Baby quail

Great blue heron

Elegant hummingbird

Hummingbird feeding

Mourning dove with gingko

Egret flying

Hawk soaring

Duck swimming

Wading egret

Mallard swimming

Duck landing

Macaw

Toucan

Tip: Flying creatures
enter and exit from
a wing or tail tip.

China knob goose

Albatross

Birds

28

Crane landing

Crane prancing

Crane ogling

Large avocet

Wading avocets

Flora & Fauna

Harp leaf

Little mum
Wild butterfly orchid

Fern leaf

Whimsical bee

Stylized wild plants

Leaf and seed medley

Maple leaf

Eucalyptus leaves and pods

Lunaria

Leaping frog

Maple leaf and
Serviceberry leaf

Half mum

Frog looking up

CHICKENS IN THE VEGETABLES *by Laura Lee Fritz, 47" x 56", 2000.*
Our chickens keep the bugs out of my garden, but they are pests themselves, eating their fill of whatever they want. This quilt is a chicken-eye view of the sumptuous feast ahead of them.

LINEN BARN JACKET *by Laura Lee Fritz, 2000.* One year I entered three quilts in a show: Alpaca Watch, Hound Dog Dreams, and The Roosters quilt. The following year I was able to go to the show myself, wearing this jacket. Because it features a sampling of characters from each of those quilts, it worked well as a calling card; everyone recognized the work.

DOVE VEST *by Laura Lee Fritz, 2000.* The flowers and leaves on the front of this vest were chosen to complement the framed dove seen on page 4.

VELVETEEN NIGHT JACKET *by Laura Lee Fritz, 2001.* What a contrast: a velvet jacket with glow-in-the-dark thread! Sometimes just a touch of quilting is all a wearable item needs to set it apart.

SHARKS AND OCTOPUS JACKET

by Laura Lee Fritz, 2000. Black and red is my uniform, and the octopus is one of my favorite creatures, the most intelligent invertebrate in the sea. In addition, I've done my share of shark fishing, so combined the fun of all these elements to make my own ultimate fishing jacket.

FISHING VEST *by Laura Lee Fritz, 2000.* I have a hard time keeping Ron in fishing vests: they get bought right off his back. I asked him to use this one plenty so it would get dirty enough that no one would want to buy it.

INDIGO GARDEN JACKET *by Laura Lee Fritz, 2000.* Using the straight line bursts to offset the flowing leaves and blossoms makes this jacket far more interesting than versions I have done with simply floral designs.

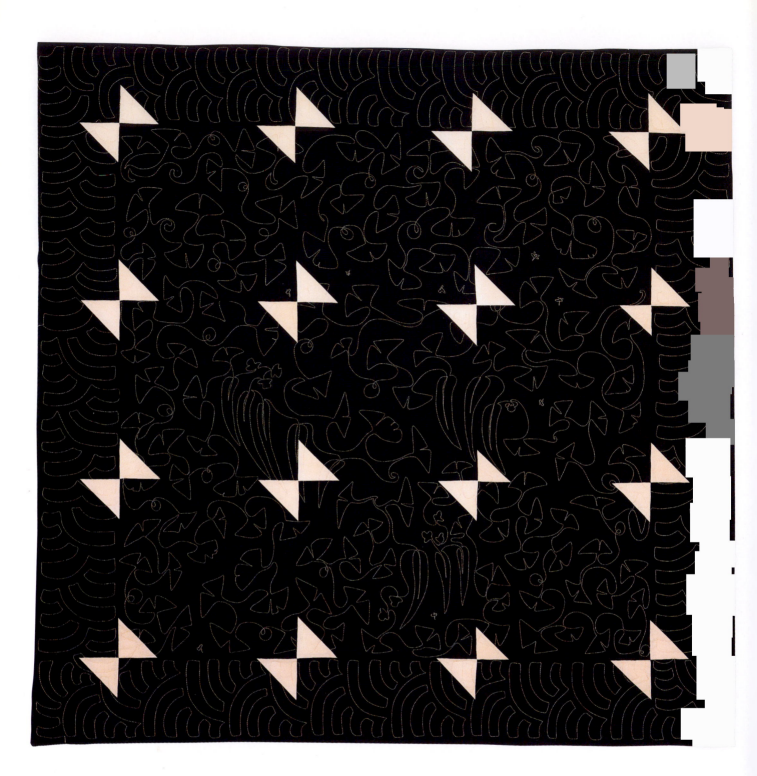

AMISH HOURGLASS *by Laura Lee Fritz, 60" square, 2000.*
This is my "remake" of a quilt in the Esprit Collection that dates to the 1880s.
I knew it needed to be quilted with the random Baptist fan, but wanted to
make it showier. I think the mix of gingko and eucalyptus leaves comes close
to engaging the same flow. After quilting, I fitted some open negative space
with flies to better balance the design.

HOUND DOG DREAMS *by Laura Lee Fritz, 70" x 76", 1997.*
I used to walk Amos, my bluetick hound, around Napa for his daily exercise, and would tell him stories of all the wild animals he would meet when we finally found our country home. I am certain he has met everyone on this quilt by now.

THE GREAT OUTDOORS *by Karen Nelson, Vacaville, CA, 50" x 67", 2000.* Karen's English Pointers are an important part of her life. She added her own line drawing of her dog to make my design more personal.

ALPACA WATCH *by Laura Lee Fritz, 60" x 51", 1999.* Our alpacas are not only an abundant source of spinnable fleece, they are fascinating neighbors.

LAURA'S CRANES *by Bernice Townsend, Rohnert Park, CA, 26" x 36", 2000.* I have always admired Bernice's hand quilting. How perfect that she was planning a crane wall quilt just as I was designing the crane quilting patterns. "The quilting on *Cranes* went really fast because of the non-stop quilting pattern," Bernice said.

GOD'S PROVIDENCE *by Meg Blau, Seattle, WA, 32" x 43", 2000.* Meg truly loves her garden, and designed this piece as a thanksgiving for the gifts of abundance she enjoys when working among her beds.

MONUMENT VALLEY VIEW *by Laura Lee Fritz, 60" x 72", 2000.*
Our dream came true: a horseback camping trip through Monument Valley. This
is a tribal park straddling Utah and Arizona, a very spiritual place for many of us.
I tried to capture the unique elements of the land and its people: the mustangs,
the Navajo ladies spinning and weaving, the Navajo-Churro sheep, petroglyphs,
and of course the magnificent monuments of weathered rock prominently rising
here and there across the valley.

Box turtle

Willow or
eucalyptus leaves

Pond turtle

Young fern

Wild orchid

Stylized woodland leaf

Tropical split leaf

Palm-like leaf

Stem of locust leaves

Wild bud

Seed

Jungle leaf and fruit

Gingko leaves with
willow leaves

Gingko leaf

Western soapberry leaf

Oak leaf

Wild lily

Trillium leaf

Wild violet

Wood sorrel blossom

Three wild irises

Whimsical beetle

Dragonfly

Simple moth

Swallowtail butterfly

Butterfly

Side view of butterfly

Mature mushroom

Young mushrooms

Fly mushroom

Mushroom stand

Strawberry patch

Poppy

Leafy branch

Fancy iris

Duck potato

Goosefoot

Lily

Bamboo, a vertical border

Iris blossom

Overall leaves

Fuchsia

Columbine

Lupine

Wheatgrass

Sunflowers

Wild Orchids

Maple leaves

Domestic Animals

Horse running

Horse walking

Horse jogging

Cat stalking 1

Cat sitting

Cat preening

Tip: Ground-based animals enter and exit from the lowest point on the ground.

Cat stalking 2

Cat lying

Cat Stretching

Cat leaping

Cat reaching

Cat walking

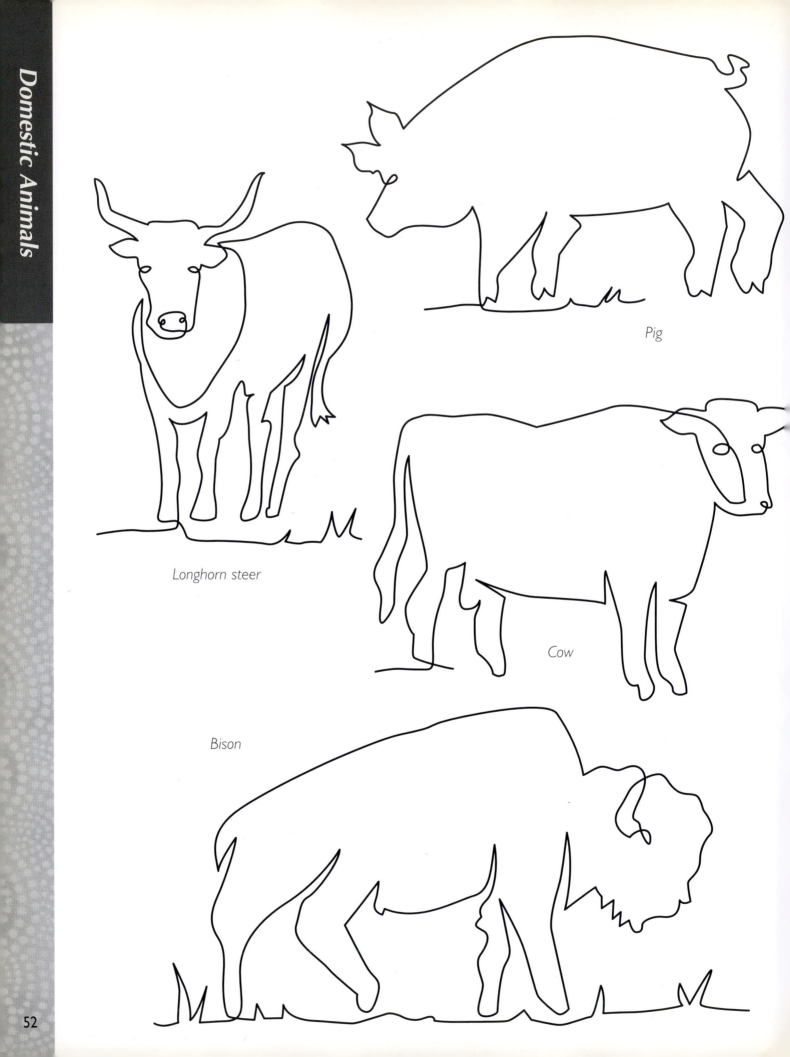

Pig

Longhorn steer

Cow

Bison

Cornish rooster

Hen

Rooster

Singing rooster

Running hound

Frolicking hound

Tracking hound

Boxer

Wolf/German shepherd

Dachsund

Scotty dog

Ram

Ewe

Ram

Little sheep

Angora goat

Angora billy goat

Young alpaca

Alpaca mom

Woodland Animals

Arctic hare

Hare sitting

Field rabbit

Kodiak bear

Running hare

Moose

Whitetail buck

Posing buck

Bounding deer

Leaping deer

Deer feeding

Mule deer doe

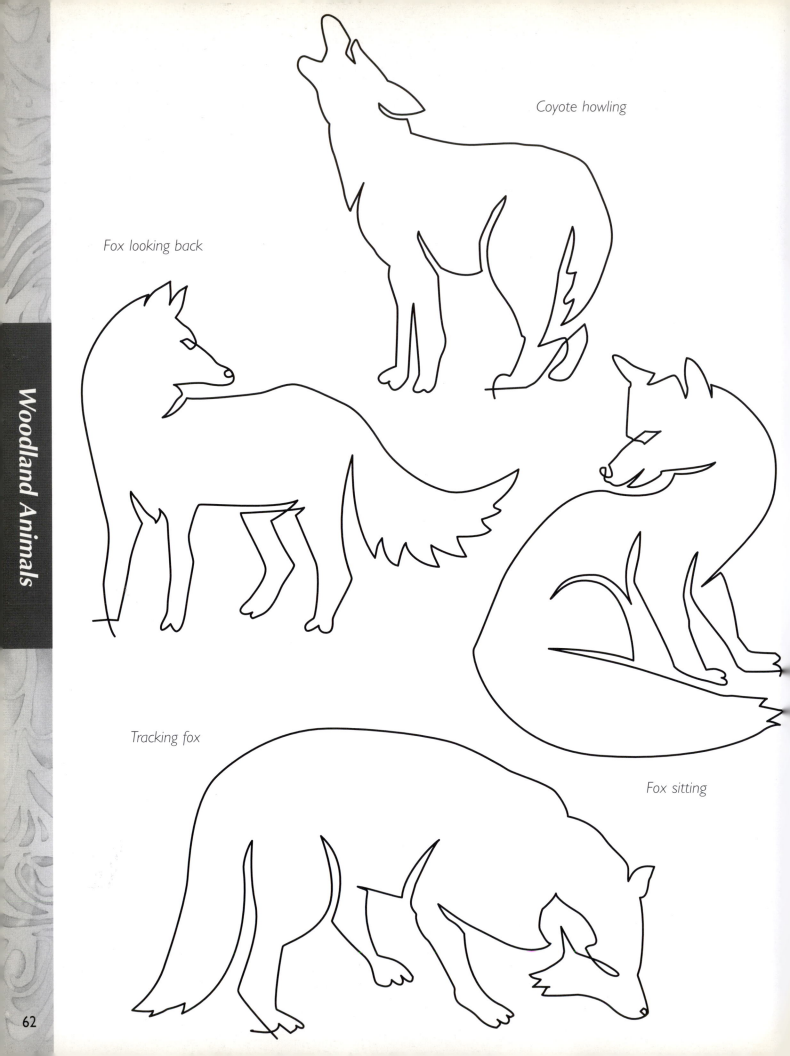

Coyote howling

Fox looking back

Tracking fox

Fox sitting

Under the Sea

Whimsical whale

Finback whale

Tiny whale

Bowhead whale

Humpback whale

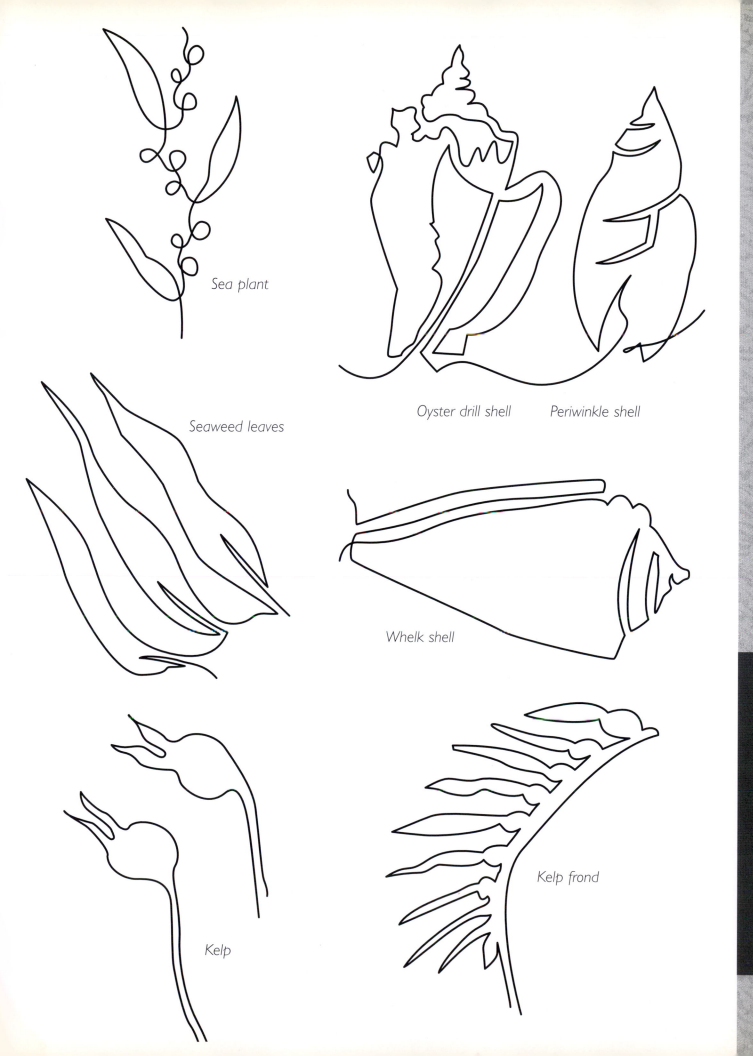

Sea plant

Seaweed leaves

Oyster drill shell   Periwinkle shell

Whelk shell

Kelp

Kelp frond

Rocking seahorse

Seahorse with seaweed

Seahorse stretching

Seahorse with sea leaves

Sea turtle

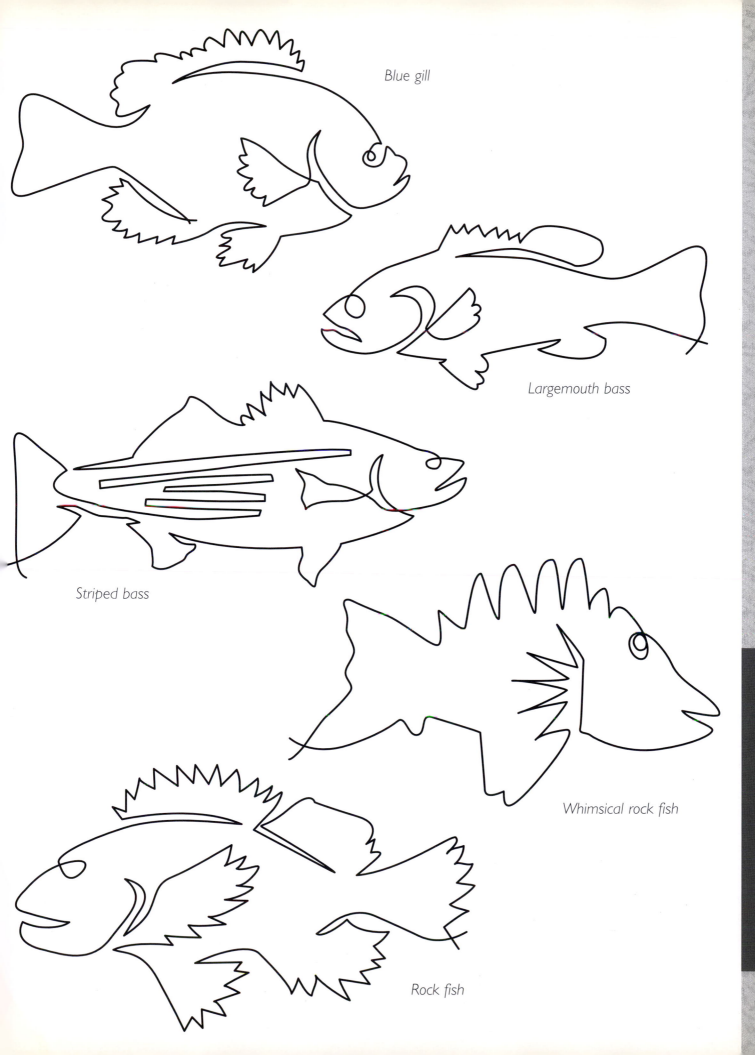

Blue gill

Largemouth bass

Striped bass

Whimsical rock fish

Rock fish

Dolphin diving

Intent dolphin

Talking dolphin

Top view of dolphin

Side view of dolphin swimming

Great white shark

Friendly shark

Tip: Swimming fish enter
and exit from the tail

Hammerhead shark

Happy shark

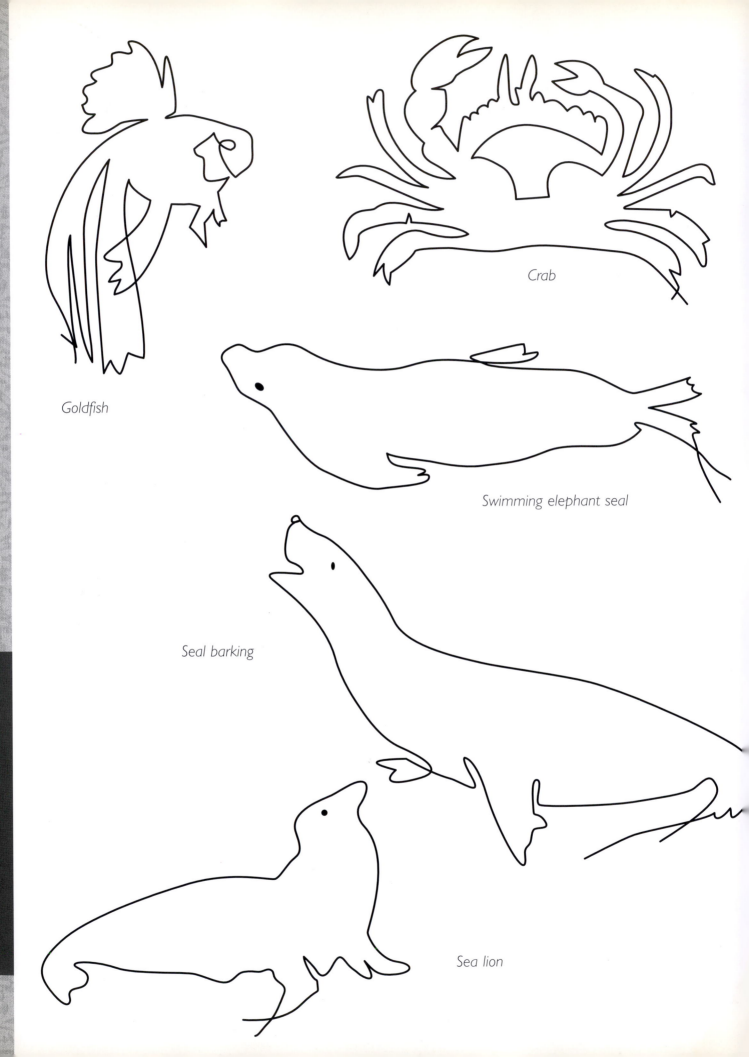

Goldfish

Crab

Swimming elephant seal

Seal barking

Sea lion

Whales in waves

Seahorse garden

Textures

Cloudy landscape with river

Split triangles

A mix of seeds and right-angle meander

Random Baptist fan

Laura's meandering

Concentric teardrops

Split circle

Right-angle meander

Beetle back

90° meander shaped like cordwood

Clouds

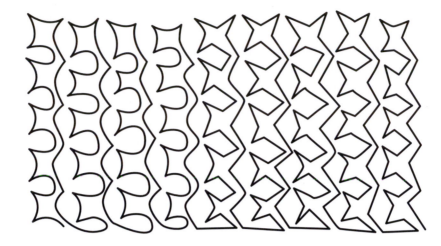

Orange peel   *Diamond plate facets*

Overall leaves

Endless mums

About the Author

Laura Lee Fritz is widely known for her hand appliqué quilts and her fanciful wholecloth quiltings filled with narrative images from the stories surrounding her life. Laura raises alpacas and rare sheep in rural Middletown, California, but slips off of the farm to teach quilting classes everywhere from her weekly class at a local college to her long-arm machine quilting classes at the annual International Quilt Festival in Houston.

Photo by Ron Paul, Spring 2001

I get my favorite ideas when I doodle with the needle. Then I trace those to get my patterns — Laura Lee Fritz

Resources

American & Efird (A & E) Inc. (Threads)
400 East Central Ave.
Mount Holly, NC 28120
800-438-0545
www.amefird.com

Gammill Quilting Systems™
1452 West Gibson
West Plains, MS 65775
800-659-8224
Gammill@townsqr.com

Hobbs Bonded Fibers
P.O. Box 2521
Waco, TX 76702
817-741-0040
usasorb@netexpress.com

Kelsul Batting
3205 Foxgrove Lane
Chesapeake, VA 23321
888-268-8664

Superior Threads
P.O. Box 1672
St. George, UT 84771
800-499-1777
www.superiorthreads.com

The Warm Company
954 E. Union Street
Seattle, WA 98122
800-234-WARM
www.warmcompany.com

YLI Corporation
161 West Main St.
Rock Hill, SC 29730
800-296-8139
www.ylicorp.com

Other Fine Books from C&T Publishing

Along the Garden Path: More Quilters and Their Gardens, Jean Wells and Valorie Wells

The Art of Machine Piecing: Quality Workmanship Through a Colorful Journey, Sally Collins

Block Magic: Over 50 Fun & Easy Blocks made from Squares and Rectangles, Nancy Johnson-Srebro

Color From the Heart: Seven Great Ways to Make Quilts with Colors You Love, Gai Perry

Color Play: Easy Steps to Imaginative Color in Quilts, Joen Wolfrom

Cotton Candy Quilts: Using Feedsacks, Vintage and Reproduction Fabrics, Mary Mashuta

Curves in Motion: Quilt Designs & Techniques, Judy B. Dales

Cut-Loose Quilts: Stack, Slice, Switch & Sew, Jan Mullen

Diane Phalen Quilts: 10 Projects to Celebrate the Seasons, Diane Phalen

Do-It-Yourself Framed Quilts: Fast, Fun & Easy Projects, Gai Perry

Easy Pieces: Creative Color Play with Two Simple Blocks, Margaret Miller

Everything Flowers: Quilts from the Garden, Jean and Valori Wells

Exploring Machine Trapunto: New Dimensions, Hari Walner

Fabric Shopping with Alex Anderson, Seven Projects to Help You: Make, Successful Choices, Build Your Confidence, Add to Your Fabric Stash, Alex Anderson

Fantastic Fabric Folding: Innovative Quilting Projects, Rebecca Wat

Flower Pounding: Quilt Projects for All Ages, Amy Sandrin & Ann Frischkorn

Freddy's House: Brilliant Color in Quilts, Freddy Moran

Free Stuff for Crafty Kids on the Internet, Judy Heim and Gloria Hansen

Free Stuff for Doll Lovers on the Internet, Judy Heim and Gloria Hansen

Free Stuff for Gardeners on the Internet, Judy Heim and Gloria Hansen

Free Stuff for Home Décor on the Internet, Judy Heim and Gloria Hansen

Free Stuff for Home Repair on the Internet, Judy Heim and Gloria Hansen

Free Stuff for Pet Lovers on the Internet, Gloria Hansen

Free Stuff for Quilters on the Internet, 3rd Ed. Judy Heim and Gloria Hansen

Free Stuff for Scrapbooking on the Internet, Judy Heim and Gloria Hansen

Free Stuff for Sewing Fanatics on the Internet, Judy Heim and Gloria Hansen

Free Stuff for Stitchers on the Internet, Judy Heim and Gloria Hansen

Free Stuff for Traveling Quilters on the Internet, Gloria Hansen

Free-Style Quilts: A "No Rules" Approach, Susan Carlson

Ghost Layers & Color Washes: Three Steps to Spectacular Quilts, Katie Pasquini Masopust

Great Lakes, Great Quilts: 12 Projects Celebrating Quilting Traditions, Marsha MacDowell

Hand Quilting with Alex Anderson: Six Projects for Hand Quilters, Alex Anderson

Heirloom Machine Quilting, Third Edition, Harriet Hargrave

In the Nursery: Creative Quilts and Designer Touches, Jennifer Sampou & Carolyn Schmitz

Laurel Burch Quilts: Kindred Creatures, Laurel Burch

Lone Star Quilts and Beyond: Projects and Inspiration, Jan Krentz

Machine Embroidery and More: Ten Step-by-Step Projects Using Border Fabrics & Beads, Kristen Dibbs

Magical Four-Patch and Nine-Patch Quilts, Yvonne Porcella

Make Any Block Any Size, Joen Wolfrom

Mastering Machine Appliqué, Harriet Hargrave

Mastering Quilt Marking: Marking Tools & Techniques, Choosing Stencils, Matching Borders & Corners, Pepper Cory

On the Surface: Thread Embellishment & Fabric Manipulation, Wendy Hill

Patchwork Persuasion: Fascinating Quilts from Traditional Designs, Joen Wolfrom

The Photo Transfer Handbook: Snap It, Print It, Stitch It!, Jean Ray Laury

Pieced Flowers, Ruth B. McDowell

Piecing: Expanding the Basics, Ruth B. McDowell

Quilted Memories: Celebrations of Life, Mary Lou Weidman

The Quilted Garden: Design & Make Nature-Inspired Quilts, Jane A. Sassaman

Quilting Back to Front: Fun & Easy No-Mark Techniques, Larraine Scouler

Quilting with Carol Armstrong: 30 Quilting Patterns, Appliqué Designs, 16 Projects, Carol Armstrong

Quilting with the Muppets: The Jim Henson Company in Association with Sesame Workshop

Quilts for Guys: 15 Fun Projects For Your Favorite Fella

Rotary Cutting with Alex Anderson: Tips, Techniques, and Projects, Alex Anderson

Rx for Quilters: Stitcher-Friendly Advice for Every Body, Susan Delaney Mech, M.D.

Setting Solutions, Sharyn Craig

Shadow Redwork™ with Alex Anderson: 24 Designs to Mix and Match, Alex Anderson

Smashing Sets: Exciting Ways to Arrange Quilt Blocks, Margaret J. Miller

Snowflakes & Quilts, Paula Nadelstern

Start Quilting with Alex Anderson, 2nd Edition: Six Projects for First-Time Quilters, Alex Anderson

Stitch 'n Flip Quilts: 14 Fantastic Projects, Valori Wells

Strips 'n Curves: A New Spin on Strip Piecing, Louisa Smith

A Thimbleberries Housewarming,:22 Projects for Quilters, Lynette Jensen

Through the Garden Gate: Quilters and Their Gardens, Jean and Valori Wells

Travels with Peaky and Spike: Doreen Speckmann's Quilting Adventures, Doreen Speckmann

Two-for-One Foundation Piecing: Reversible Quilts and More, Wendy Hill

Wild Birds: Designs for Appliqué & Quilting, Carol Armstrong

Wildflowers: Designs for Appliqué & Quilting, Carol Armstrong

For more information write for a free catalog:
C&T Publishing, Inc.
P.O. Box 1456
Lafayette, CA 94549
(800) 284-1114
e-mail: ctinfo@ctpub.com
website: www.ctpub.com

For quilting supplies:
Cotton Patch Mail Order
3405 Hall Lane, Dept. CTB
Lafayette, CA 94549
(800) 835-4418
(925) 283-7883
e-mail: quiltusa@yahoo.com
website: www.quiltusa.com